Language Teaching Course Design:

Trends and Issues

Curriculum Development Series 1

Language Teaching Course Design: Trends and Issues

David Nunan

National Curriculum Resource Centre
1985

Published and distributed by
National Curriculum Resource Centre
5th Floor, Renaissance Centre
127 Rundle Mall
Adelaide, South Australia 5000.

ISBN 0 7243 7426 4

© *Commonwealth of Australia 1985*

Printed by D. J. Woolman, Government Printer, South Australia

National Curriculum Resource Centre

The National Curriculum Resource Centre was established by the Education Branch, Department of Immigration and Ethnic Affiars, in 1984. It is located within the Adelaide College of Technical and Further Education.

The NCRC was set up to provide a curriculum and professional development service for the Adult Migrant Education Program. This program is administered across Australia by a variety of state educational bodies.

The functions of the Centre are as follows:

1. The provision of a materials and syllabus development service for state bodies within the Adult Migrant Education Program.
2. Specific materials and curricula development projects and associated production.
3. The provision of advice, expertise and support for materials and curricula development.
4. The dissemination of information on current international developments in the field of English as a Second Language materials and curricula development.

At present, the NCRC is involved in the production of materials on a national basis, and the provision of advice for state-based materials and syllabus development projects. It is actively involved in teacher development, producing videotapes and conducting in-service seminars and workshops on issues of professional concern. The Centre is also the publisher of *Prospect*, the journal of the Adult Migrant Education Program.

Curriculum Development Series

This is the first in a series of curriculum development hand-books published by the National Curriculum Resource Centre. These handbooks are designed to assist teachers in the planning and implementation of their courses.

Each handbook, with the exception of this initial overview volume, will provide teachers with current perspectives on a chosen area of curriculum design. They are intended to provide practical assistance, and will therefore focus on techniques and methods which teachers can put to immediate use in the planning and development of courses and materials.

Future publications in the series will look in detail at practical techniques for needs analysis and objective setting, evaluation, teacher-produced materials and developing alternative learning modes.

Contents

List of Figures

Introduction

A great many changes have taken place within the field of language teaching over the last ten or fifteen years. Some of these changes have been extremely desirable, others less so. However, taken together, they have had the effect of transforming the field.

Understandably, the giddy pace of change has left many teachers completely bemused. There is a feeling that such changes as have occurred are fragmentary, contradictory, and that they are pulling the profession in different directions. Such perceptions are understandable at a time of rapid change.

However, most of the changes which have occurred can be seen to have evolved out of beliefs about language, the learner and language learning which share a number of underlying philosophical principles. The most important of these were first related to the Adult Migrant Education Program by Ingram (1979).

In this handbook, I should like to reexamine some of the principles articulated by Ingram and others, and to conduct a general exploration of those issues relating to syllabus design, materials development and methodology which are of current interest to the language teaching profession. I hope that such an exploration will help bring teachers up to date with what is happening at a professional level both within the AMEP and beyond, and that it will also assist in the formulation of a coherent view of AMEP philosophy and policy. Despite the different currents and trends, I hope to be able to demonstrate that it is possible to extract from these an underlying ideology which has a reasonable degree of coherence. As Ingram states:

> In all teaching, if learning is not to be dissipated in fragmented or desultory activities, it is essential that the total program be coherent and integrated. This is particularly important where . . .emphasis falls on learning through use and on responding to learners' needs. (1979:A10).

1 Objectives of the Adult Migrant Education Program (AMEP)

From documents such as the AMEP Handbook (1984), the following points can be seen to summarise the philosophy of the Program itself.

1. To enable learners to gain enough English to function in the community, to acquire the skills necessary to become independent and autonomous learners, and to develop sufficient English to gain access to educational and other community services.

2. To develop learning arrangements which encourage self-help, individualisation and promote a view of language as a tool for achieving life goals rather than as an end in itself.

3. To develop a methodology which takes a functional approach to language, exploits 'authentic' materials, sees genuine interaction outside the classroom as essential to language development, familiarises learners with Australian culture, is based on learners needs, establishes clear objectives, capitalises on learning strategies already acquired by learners, and encourages self-reliance and self-assessment.

From the above, it is obvious that the Program is moving in the direction of learner-centred needs-based courses in which the learner is encouraged away from dependence on the teacher. At the same time there is a parallel pressure on teachers to become more self-directed and independent, particularly in developing their own programs and materials.

2 Syllabus Design

In order to provide a framework to integrate some of the directions indicated above, and also to allow for a more detailed discussion of current developments in the professional area, the following syllabus design model is proposed.

Figure 1: Elements in a Process Syllabus

This model differs in a number of significant respects from traditional models such as those proposed by Tyler (1949), and Taba (1962). To begin with, it can be used to guide ongoing as well as initial syllabus development. The traditional model is only useful in initial syllabus development, that is, in the specification of course elements up to the point at which the course is to be delivered. However, much of the most valuable course development occurs while a course is actually being taught. A syllabus model ought to reflect this fact. It is for this reason that the teaching/learning process is placed at the centre of the model. The third thing that differentiates the model is its comprehensiveness. Traditional models tend to restrict themselves to objectives specification, content selection, grading and evaluation. It is felt by some syllabus designers that there ought to be a rigid separation between syllabus design and methodology, in other words, that considerations of what to teach ought to be kept separate from how to teach. Such a separation has led in the past to such aberrations as the teaching of courses whose input was specified in functional/ notional terms through an audiolingual methodology.

In the model proposed here, all the elements are in interaction and each may influence the other. Objectives may be modified, altered or added to during the course of the teaching/learning process. Decisions about what goes on in the classroom will be influenced, not only by prespecified objectives, materials and activities, but also by needs, constraints (what is feasible, say in the learning mode and environment) and by the evaluation feedback which emerges during the course itself.

This model and its various elements is significant for the classroom teacher because the role of the teacher has changed quite dramatically over the last ten years. In the early seventies, most teachers within the Adult Migrant Education Program were likely to have been using *Situational English,* and, in consequence, to have had comparatively little control over most elements in the design model. The teacher's domain was seen to be responsibility for orchestrating, pacing and presenting materials and activities produced by someone else. This is not to say that teachers had no part to play in setting goals, developing materials, course evaluation and so on; simply that developments over the years (such as the abandoning of set coursebooks) have created a situation where teachers have a much greater responsibility than hitherto for making decisions relating to each of the elements and stages within the syllabus design process. This is particularly so for areas such as goal setting, needs analysis, learning mode and environment and evaluation, areas where the teacher was largely dictated to by course designers and educational administrators. Given greater responsibility, teachers need guidance on current developments in these areas. The rest of this handbook is devoted to setting out some of these developments.

3 Needs Analysis

Most teachers working within the Program are aware of the current emphasis being given to the place of needs analysis in course design. The major statement in this area is that by Brindley (1984) on needs analysis and objective setting within the Program, a statement which will not be reiterated here.

Within the model outlined above, most of the teacher-based needs analysis will take the form of informal monitoring by the teacher during course delivery. This informal monitoring is in contrast to the extensive pre-course analysis suggested by people such as Munby (1978) which is, in fact, conducted without ongoing consultation with the learner. Such analysis might be sufficient for initial course development, but there is something almost contradictory about needs analysis which does not involve the learner. Of course the degree to which pre-course analysis can be conducted will depend to a large extent on the experience of the teacher with the type of student for which the course is being developed. Extensive pre-course analysis is also of little use in centres where, because of numbers, alternative learning arrangements are not practicable.

Establishing the learning needs of the individual student can only come about through the often lengthy process of getting to know each individual student. Once again, a process syllabus allows for recognition of the fact that this sort of qualitative analysis develops over time. In fact, students sometimes go to a former rather than current teacher to articulate needs because they know the former best and relate to them most intimately.

A number of writers on needs analysis pay some attention to the distinction between 'objective' and 'subjective' needs. Brindley (1984) suggests that:

5

'objective' needs are those which can be diagnosed by teachers on the basis of the analysis of personal data about learners along with information about their language proficiency and patterns of language use . . . 'subjective' needs (which are often 'wants', 'desires', 'expectations' or other psychological manifestations of a lack) cannot be diagnosed as easily. (p.31)

Further on, Brindley identifies objective needs with content (i.e. linguistic input) and subjective needs with learning process, and draws support for this view from Widdowson (1981) who differentiates between goal orientated needs (which relate to terminal behaviour) and process-orientated needs (relating to the means of achieving that terminal behaviour). However, it is disputable whether, in fact, he is making the same point as Brindley. Brindley is distinguishing between two different types of analysis, whereas Widdowson is questioning the postulation of a direct one-to-one correlation between input and methodology. Widdowson's point is taken up again later, in the section on input specification.

There are, in fact, two different dimensions here. One of these is the objective/subjective dimension, the other is the content/methodology dimension. These are represented in Figure 2.

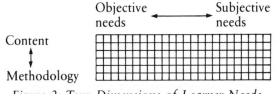

Figure 2: Two Dimensions of Learner Needs.

While objective needs analysis and content are commonly linked, as are subjective needs and methodology, the diagram demonstrates that it is, in fact, also possible to have a content/subjective needs dimension (learners deciding what they want to learn) and a methodology/objective needs dimension (teachers deciding how content might best be learned). The dimensions themselves are represented as a series of graduations rather than discrete categories.

Richterich (1983) has been in the forefront of work on needs analysis. For him, the identification of language needs is an essential prerequisite to the task of setting objectives. He states that in order to determine objectives which accurately reflect the language needs of the learners it is obligatory:

> to acquire better understanding of the characteristics, capabilities and resources of the target groups concerned, in order to identify their language needs and select the objectives, content and curricula which will satisfy them. (p.2)

He discussed three criticisms of needs analysis. These are as follows:

(i) The concept is ambiguous and can be conceived of in terms which are either too narrow or too broad to be useful.

(ii) The learner is unaware of his needs, and generally unable to express them except in vague terms. Richterich voices the added concern that specifying needs does not mean these will automatically be translated into classroom practice, that 'information gathered is rarely exploited satisfactorily in the day-to-day work of the classroom, where it comes up against all sorts of institutional obstacles and against resistance, routine and obtuseness'. (p.3)

(iii) If needs analysis and objective setting are carried out too rigidly, they will, in fact, block any changes that may become necessary during program delivery.

While Richterich accepts these criticisms to a certain extent, he looks to the practical benefits of needs analysis on course design and methodology as justification for carrying it out. He suggests that it should also be kept in proportion, that 'the identification of needs can only be one tool among others for obtaining relative, partial, temporary and circumstantial information which will help us make choices and take decisions without any pretension to scientific, definitive truth' (p.3). He also suggests that 'scientific' approaches are unnecessary, that:

> willingness to make changes where possible within his zone of influence, the conviction that the pupils should also have their say since their studies are their own, a little imagination and knowledge of possible practices, no more is needed to make language needs identification an educational tool that everyone can handle. (p.9).

A major reason for conducting a needs analysis is to provide a specification of input which is relevant to the needs of a given learner or group of learners. If it were possible or desirable to teach the entire system of the target language, then needs analysis would not be necessary. We teach a sample of the target system and assume that learning transfer will take care of the rest. Widdowson (1983), in an investigation into specific as opposed to general purpose courses, suggests that specific purpose courses are designed to provide the restricted competence needed to cope with a circumscribed set of needs and can therefore be equated with training, while general purpose courses are aimed at producing general competence and are therefore to be equated with the concept of education. In other words, specific purpose courses are aimed at getting students to perform the sort of tasks they have been specifically taught but not necessarily anything else; learning transfer is not assumed. The assumption in the argument is that needs based courses are unlikely to promote transfer of learning, and are consequently unlikely to take the learner in the direction of general competence.

Almost immediately, however, Widdowson acknowledges the fact that this conclusion is an oversimplification, that there is a continuum from non-transferable learning to transferable learning along which all courses will reside. He says that:

> although certain occupational courses might be located at the training end of the spectrum, the most specific end, this does not mean that learners will derive from them no educational benefit and will be deprived of the chance to develop communicative capacity . . . the trainee, in acquiring this required (restricted) competence, may well have developed at the same time a potential for later exploitation in other areas of activity. The learner may always go beyond the goals of the course of instruction, just as he or she may always fall short of them (p.11).

This admission weakens his case.

Pedagogically, the most powerful argument in favour of needs-based courses is a motivational one. The need to motivate students has become a cliché. One way of improving motivation is to orientate content towards those areas that most interest learners and which are perceived by them as being most relevant, and to develop methodologies which enhance the learner's self-concept rather than destroying it. It is also in line with the principles of adult learning articulated by Knowles (1983) and others.

From the perspective of the AMEP, there is a need for teachers to develop and document procedures for needs analysis. Recently it has become apparent that many teachers feel they lack the necessary skills in this area. There is also a perception that most analysis carried out is fairly superficial and that the last thing learners need is to be subjected to yet more questionnaires.

As already indicated, needs analysis can be conceived of in two stages. Stage 1, the objective needs analysis, is that carried out before the beginning of a course, and involves consideration of both input and methodology, that is, consideration of what the learners encounter in terms of linguistic product, and the learning process through which the product is to be achieved. Stage 2 is the subjective needs analysis, which is conducted during the course of program delivery. This stage involves, as far as possible, the collaboration of the learner in making decisions about the 'what' and 'how' of the course. It is this second stage which potentially is of most value, and therefore of most interest at the present time, and the major task confronting teachers and administrators is in devising ways of encouraging learners to articulate their needs and to participate in the process of course development and modification. A sample interview form used for the collection of subjective data at the Pennington Migrant Education Centre in South Australia is attached as Appendix A.

4 Setting Goals

An awareness of the need for teachers to spend time setting appropriate goals for their courses became widespread during the seventies. Prior to this time, it was generally assumed that the teacher's task was to teach the target language in its entirety. One started from scratch and went as far as was possible given the constraints of resources and time. One was also concerned almost exclusively with teaching the grammatical system of the language.

The shortcomings of this view became apparent when language teachers, applied linguists and course designers began to look beyond grammar for insights into the nature of language. The incorporation of functional/notional principles into course design and the development of communicative methods in the classroom were reflections of a broader view of the nature of language and language learning. Language was no longer seen as a discrete grammatical system existing in isolation, but as a set of resources and options for achieving a variety of goals outside the language classroom. In other words, it was perceived as a tool rather than as an end in itself.

Taking a functional orientation had a number of implications for course design. Functionalism suggests that language exists to fulfil a variety of purposes. It is not unreasonable that perhaps these purposes ought to be taught in class, that students ought to be taught, not only what the target system is, but how it is used. Given the fact that different learners will have different purposes and goals, it would seem that the first stages in course design should involve specifying purposes and goals. The end result will be much greater diversity between and within courses as teachers attempt to cater for a variety of needs.

Within the AMEP, some idea of the diversity of offerings can be gauged from the titles of courses. The following have been selected at random from course and program reports:

Safety in the Workplace
Advanced Level Comprehension and Discourse Skills
The Language of Childbirth
Language Skills for Dressmakers
Developing Basic Literacy Skills

From a survey of courses such as these it can be seen that teachers and course planners start from a number of different points in setting course goals. The course can reflect the sorts of uses to which the target language will be put, the contexts and situations in which it will be used, the target clientele, the skills that will be developed and the level at which the courses will be conducted.

There are some teachers who reject the need for specifying goals in any but the most general terms, arguing that the task for all learners, whether they be illiterate Indo-Chinese grandmothers or post-graduate Polish engineers, is the internalisation of the underlying linguistic system of the target language. These teachers argue that setting different goals for different learners is unnecessary.

This language-centred, rather than learner-centred argument is untenable on a number of counts. In the first place, as has already been seen, no course can hope to teach the totality of the linguistic system. Therefore, one must make selections. It seems not unreasonable to make those selections on the basis of the perceived needs and interests of the learners. Secondly, those who talk in terms of the internalisation of the linguistic system seem to overlook the fact that language is not content free. For learners with immediate or clearly defined needs (such as pregnant women who are going into hospitals where English is the medium of instruction), courses should provide language which is immediately useful and which also provides a basis for the internalisation of the underlying linguistic system.

Recent research suggests that all learners acquire this underlying linguistic system in a fixed developmental sequence (Johnston, 1984). The provision of courses which relate to the needs and interests of the learners, in which the language is presented in rich, meaningful and relevant contexts, and in which there are clear links between the language and the purposes to which it will be put, should provide the most favourable conditions for this developmental process to occur.

The goals of special purpose courses are generally established by the teacher or course designer before the course itself begins. With general English courses there is much more latitude to involve learners in the process of establishing goals. This process can be as simple as asking students which of the macro-skills they wish to focus on or which content areas they would like to cover from a given list. Brindley (1984) provides an example of an ad hoc method of establishing broad goals for general English courses. The procedure, taken from Shaw (1982) involves providing learners with a list of general options which they rank in order of preference. These are then arranged into a hierarchy through a process of negotiation between learners. The general objectives suggested in the example include such things as understanding English grammar better, writing English more fluently and correctly, understanding radio and T.V. better, knowing more about Australian culture, reading and understanding newspapers better, and learning how to spell better.

An alternative suggestion would be to produce skills/content grids. These would allow students to specify the general skills they would like to focus on and the content areas in which they would like to work.

Content Areas

	Health	Newspapers	Shopping	Australian Culture
Skills				
Listening				
Reading				
Speaking				
Writing				
Vocabulary				
Grammar				

Figure 3: Example of Skills/Content Grid for Goal Setting

Setting broad course goals can either precede or be conducted hand in hand with needs analysis. In general, the goals of a course indicate the general direction in which the course is heading, which of the macro-skills are being emphasised, whether the course is to have a special purpose orientation and so on. As with needs analysis, it is possible to make modifications to the goals of the course during program delivery, although it is unlikely that such modifications will be major ones. It is unlikely, for instance, that a course established to develop advanced listening skills will end up concentrating on the development of reading or writing (although such an eventuality need not be completely ruled out). A recent advanced ESP course for technicians, which started out with a technical language orientation ended up, after the students had been on work placement, concentrating on the development of casual conversation skills. This came about as a result of student articulated needs as a result of their workplace experiences. Most modifications to course goals are not as radical as this, however, and any modifications as a result of ongoing needs analysis can be incorporated into the overall original intention of the course.

5   Specifying Input

Once the general goals of a course have been set, the next task is to specify the ways in which these goals will be achieved. This is often a difficult task, and one which, over the years, has caused a great deal of contention and controversy. Much of the controversy revolved around whether input ought to be specified in grammatical or functional/notional terms. The formal/functional debate, which is still being waged, has been well documented, and the pros and cons of one procedure rather than another will not be entered into here. (For recent discussion on the implications of the debate for syllabus design see Bell 1981, or Yalden 1983). Most teachers and course designers recognise the need to specify input along more than one dimension. This has resulted in such initiatives as the Staging Approach which will be described later.

An attempt has been made to overcome the fragmentation which resulted from the form/function controversy by taking input specifications back one step, and reintroducing the notion of performance objectives. The use of performance or (as they were then called) behavioural objectives came in for a good deal of criticism in the early seventies, when the shortcomings of behaviourist psychology were being documented. Like programmed instruction, objectives had been closely associated with behaviourism, and so it was not unexpected that a decline in both behaviourism and the objectives movement should go hand in hand. While the criticisms of the objectives approach as it was conceived and developed in the sixties and early seventies are valid, it is possible to develop an alternative conceptualisation which largely obviates these earlier criticisms. This alternative conceptualisation will be outlined shortly.

The best known work on the application of performance objectives to language teaching is that by Valette and Disick (1972), who suggest that such objectives differ from other sorts of objectives in that output rather than input should be stressed and that this output should be stated in terms of student performance. Having determined output, one can then go ahead and specify the input likely to achieve this. Specifying student output as a first step has a number of advantages. It focuses on the ultimate goal and therefore assists the teacher in developing a program which relates to student needs, it acts as a guide in the selection of materials and activities and it provides a means of evaluation.

Many criticisms have been made of the objectives approach, and there is no room here to detail each of these. Two of the more important, which I should like to comment on, concern the level of specificity required for setting objectives, and the relationship between objectives and the learning process.

The specificity problem arose out of the behaviourist concern to teach, and therefore to prespecify, every single thing a student need learn or be able to do in order to achieve a final learning outcome. Of course, as soon as one tries to do this, one is faced with the task of developing huge banks of learning objectives. MacDonald-Ross (1975), one of the major critics of the objectives movement, states that:

> The level of specificity problem is the most cruel dilemma faced by the advocate of behavioural objectives. It runs like this: If you have only a few general objectives they are easy to remember and handle, but too vague and ambiguous. But if you try to eliminate ambiguity by splitting down the objectives and qualifying the conditions of performance, then the list becomes impossibly long (p.368).

However, if one abandons behaviourism for a cognitive-learning perspective, one is in a position to place much greater trust in the ability of the learner to develop skills which have not been taught from skills which have through a process of transfer. After all, if transfer can not be assumed to occur, learning can hardly be said to have taken place.

Gronlund (1981), deals with the levels of specificity problem by suggesting that general objectives be specified for a course, and that these be underpinned by a number of specific performance objectives which are not exhaustive, but which provide examples of the sorts of things the learner needs to be able to do to demonstrate mastery of the general objectives.

The following example should help to clarify the distinction between goals, general objectives, and specific objectives:

Goal: To develop discourse processing skills relating to written tests

General Objective: Comprehends textual relationships

Specific Objectives: Traces identity chains
Identifies points of ellipsis
Assigns antecedents to anaphoric reference items

Here it can be seen that the performance objectives are a list of examples of the sorts of things a learner would need to be able to do to demonstrate mastery of the general objective.

The other way of avoiding the proliferation of objectives is to keep them content free as far as is possible. It was the tendency in the sixties to tie objectives to content which was partially responsible for the fragmentation and proliferation of objectives. One of the problems with content-free objectives is their vagueness. One ends up with objectives such as the following:

> Pass on to a third person information given orally
> Ask a number of related questions in order to obtain information and/or advice
> (Royal Society of Arts, 1984)

While it is not always possible to keep language learning objectives content free, (when, for instance, one is teaching numbers, the alphabet and the time), it is possible to develop grids which relate objectives and content without irrevocably tying one to the other. (For sample objective/content grids, see Appendix B).

Another reason why objectives fell into disfavour was that a direct link was assumed between the objectives and what actually went on in the classroom. Thus, in special purpose courses aimed at, say, developing skills in reading professional journals, most class time was actually spent in carrying out the terminal task, that is, in doing 'reading' exercises with the professional journals. However there is no reason why rehearsing the final performance is necessarily the only or even the best way of reaching the goal. Indeed, there may be very good reasons for not spending a great deal of class time in actually carrying out terminal tasks related to performance objectives. The example just cited is a case in point. Reading professional journals can be extremely dull and boring. The need to maintain interest and motivation may therefore suggest less direct pathways to the objective.

There may be other good reasons for avoiding a performance based approach to learning exercises and activities, particularly when it comes to the development of interpersonal attitudinal skills. There was something artificial about early functional coursebooks which presented students with a list of phrases and minimal contextual support and told them to practise 'disagreeing politely'. It may well be that the best we can do is to let students develop their comprehension of attitudinal and interpersonal functions through a study of native speaker performance. There is, in fact, evidence which suggest that speaking skills develop as a result of comprehension training rather than production (Winitz 1981).

Recently, some course designers have suggested that syllabuses can be specified exclusively in terms of what the learners are to do in the classroom, and that the specification of input can be ignored.

Prabhu (1984), for instance, points out the lack of congruence between the statement of linguistic input and the means of achieving learning objectives; that is, the lack of congruence between syllabus specifications and methodology. While Prabhu provides some valuable insights into what have come to be known as procedural or process-based syllabuses, his comments do not invalidate the adoption of an objective approach, they merely reinforce the point being made here, that problems are encountered when a direct link between objectives and teaching/learning process is assumed.

Having specified objectives, and the content areas to which they relate, one can then proceed to specify the linguistic realisations of these objectives. Most recent courses such as, for example, the Cambridge English Course, take a multidimensional approach, specifying and integrating functions, notions and structures into their syllabus design. This makes the task for the syllabus designer much more complex than hitherto because he/she must select, sequence and integrate vertically (deciding which grammatical and functional items will be taught before which) and horizontally (deciding which structures, functions, etc. will be integrated and taught together).

Yalden (1983), in her discussion of the problem of interrelating syllabus components, suggests that there are basically six different ways of specifying input from a communicative perspective. These are as follows:

> Type 1: *Structural/Functional*: This is the old structural syllabus with the addition of a functional component. There is no attempt to integrate structures and functions, and these are taught separately.

Type 2: Structures and Functions: Here, structural progression is still the organising principle, but, unlike Type 1, notional, functional and situational components are integrated into the course from the beginning.

Type 3: Variable Focus: In this type, focus shifts from structural to functional to situation based exercises and activities as the competence of the learner increases.

Type 4: Functional: For this type 'objectives are stated primarily in terms of communicative functions, not in terms of linguistic items or in terms of ideational content, although these components are included and sometimes obscure the purpose of the syllabus design'.

Type 5: Fully Notional: Under this category, Yalden lumps together the approach of Wilkins (1976), Van Ek (1975), and Munby (1978).

Type 6: Fully Communicative: Here the learner, working with authentic materials, determines the direction of the syllabus.

This particular type is justified in the following terms:

> If we focus on communicative skills, we will inevitably develop most areas of linguistic competence. If we focus on linquistic skills only, or even primarily, we risk failing to deal with a large part of communicative competence, however that may be defined. To accomplish the former, Allwright advocates having the teacher's management activities directed exclusively at involving the learners in solving communication problems. In so doing, language learning would take care of itself (pp.117-118).

Yalden goes on to say that this final type takes us so far away from the concept of a well-formulated plan of action that it is difficult to think of it as an approach to syllabus design at all.

One of the most comprehensive sets of specifications for syllabus development is that produced by the Council of Europe under the editorship of Van Ek (1975), and published as the Threshold Level. This work specifies communicative situations, settings, roletypes, topics, functions, notions, linguistic exponents and lexis. It is an extremely comprehensive document. It should be noted, however, that the Threshold Level is not a syllabus but an inventory. Moreover, it is an inventory designed for a specific group of learners, that is, adults learning language in a European context for social and professional reasons. It may or may not be suitable for other learning contexts.

Without doubt, the most comprehensive comparable inventory for the Australian context must be the AMEP On-Arrival Content Suggestion Frames which specify situations, topics, functions, notions, exponents and lexis for migrants and refugees. The Frames have existed for a number of years, but have not really been exploited to their full potential in the development of courses and materials. There are a number of reasons for this. A major reason is probably the gap as perceived by classroom teachers between the content suggestions themselves and the classroom. In other words, there is perceived to be a problem in translating the material in the frames into a syllabus and then into materials, exercises and activities for the classroom. Another problem is the fact that large numbers of recent refugees have much lower competence than those who were in AMES programs at the time the Frames were devised. There is a perception among teachers working with such students, that the suggestions in the Frames are too difficult for their students.

In working with inventories such as the Threshold Level and the AMEP Frames, the syllabus designer or teacher must make selections and decide how these are to be integrated. Some groupings, such as the following, suggest themselves quite naturally, others are more arbitrary.

Grammar	Function	Notion	Exponent
Subject	Identification	Identification	I'm George
pronouns	of self and		
Verb 'be'	others		He's Quoc
			She's Linn

Some teachers have found that it is unnecessary to specify grammatical items, that by working from lists of functional-notional and topical areas and by devising activities from these which they believe to be interesting and meaningful for their students, the core grammar is covered quite naturally. The question then becomes one of deciding whether and to what extent the student's attention ought to be drawn to the various discrete grammatical points; whether, in fact, an explicit or implicit methodological procedure ought to be followed.

Few, if any, of the function and/or topical courses developed so far have been able to derive a set of principles for selecting and grading input which is not arbitrary. Krashen and Terrell (1983), for instance, have adopted a non-grammatical topical procedure for specifying the syllabus in the 'Natural Approach'. Their input selection is based on notional topics, and situations are specified in which these will be used.

For example:

Family, Friends and Daily Activities
Topics

1. Family and relatives	4. Daily activities
2. Physical states	5. Holiday and vacation activities
3. Emotional states	6. Pets

Situations
1. Introducing, meeting people
2. Visiting relatives

It can be seen from the above example that the way the various syllabus components are arranged is quite arbitrary e.g. the association of emotional states, daily activities and pets. This may not necessarily be a problem. However, it does mean that associations are likely to be relevant only for a given group. If this is so, it is the classroom teacher who is going to have to take the major responsibility for selecting and arranging input based on his/her knowledge of the interests of the students and their general level of competence.

In adopting a non-linear selection criterion, Krashen and Terrell are not rejecting the idea that students need to acquire the grammatical system of the target language. On the contrary, they assert that by following the syllabus of the Natural Approach, the students actually acquire more grammar:

> ... focusing on communicative goals provides far more comprehensible meaningful input and encourages more language acquisition than basing the course on grammar. If we provide discussion, hence input, over a wide variety of topics while providing communicative goals, the necessary grammatical structures are automatically provided in the input. (p.72)

Whether students automatically internalise these grammatical structures without having them taught is one of the great imponderables of current language teaching theory and research and will be discussed later. The answer is likely to be a qualified one. Some students do seem to be able to benefit from the explicit teaching of structures, while at the same time internalising other aspects of the language without explicit teaching. Other learners are able to internalise the language without any explicit teaching whatsoever. It seems not only are students different in terms of preferred learning styles, but the same students have different preferred learning styles at different times and for different aspects of the language. Certainly more and more theorists and practitioners are beginning to question the psycholinguistic reality of Krashen's strict separation between acquisition and learning (see for example, Rivers, 1983; Strevens, 1984).

The above discussion, in which questions of input selection become entwined with the issue of how it should be taught, illustrates the difficulty of separating syllabus design (the 'what') from methodology (the 'how') in trying to come to practical and workable solutions to course design and implementation problems.

Once functional courses and materials began to appear under the title of 'communicative' language learning and teaching, a number of commentators, particularly those with a background in discourse analysis, began to question whether, in fact, these courses were 'communicative'. The hunt for a definition of 'communication' and 'communicative' was on.

One of the most perceptive critics, Widdowson (1979), questioned whether static lists of language functions were any more communicative than lists of grammatical points. He made the observation that functions do not, as a general rule, exist in isolation, and that communicative language use is a dynamic process in which meanings are negotiated and in which language functioning is intimately connected with the context in which it is used.

The fact that the term 'communicative' is problematic, meaning different things to different people, has not made the task of communicative syllabus design any easier. Trim (1983), who sees the current controversy as part of a long historical process, states that:

> those who follow the communicative approach are sufficiently diverse to evoke, between them, these incompatible criticisms. It is possible to stretch the concept of communication to cover multiple-choice single-point grammatical testing as the candidate 'communicating' his knowledge of grammar to the examiner. (p.71)

Hopefully, few current classroom teachers would subscribe to such a poverty stricken conceptualisation of what communication is all about.

The Lothian Region's graded objectives project (Clark and Hamilton, 1984) sees communication as the utilisation of language which transcends formal practice and which may involve the integrated use of more than one skill. Classroom activities are judged as more or less communicative according to whether:

—the purpose transcends formal practice
—there are participants involved and their relationships are clear
—'texts' are used for the purposes for which they were produced
—there is an information, opinion or affect gap
—there is a degree of unpredictability between input and output
—the communication conforms to real life norms of discourse coherence (p.5).

One of the problems faced by teachers who are attracted to new ideas (either through boredom or dissatisfaction with the results they currently obtain) is deciding on the degree to which they adopt the new ideas. Do they abandon what they currently do and embrace the new ideas wholesale, or do they attempt some sort of integration.

Most proponents of communicative language teaching advocate some sort of integration. Wilkins (1976), maintained that his ideas for notional syllabuses should be seen as complementary to current practice, and that they would probably be best suited to a post-beginner level. According to Clark and Hamilton (1984),

> some people have thought that communication and the communicative approach should now replace all the other things we have traditionally done in the classroom. This is not our view. What we aim to do is to add the communicative dimension to the other things that have proved successful in classroom language learning. (p.5)

This, they add, will involve the development of communicative and linguistic skills and strategies.

It should be kept in mind that there are, of course, others who advocate the abandonment of much or all of what has traditionally been done in the classroom if it is out of step with their particular philosophy of language development and learning.

Teachers of low level and/or low ability groups have a particular problem in deciding the degree to which a communicative approach can be implemented with learners who have not yet mastered the basic morphological and syntactic patterns of the language.

Most of the materials and courses based on communicative language learning principles are designed for students who have reached a pre-intermediate level and who therefore have a base grammar to operate from. Should the teacher of beginners decide that it is feasible to incorporate some of the new ideas, he/she must then decide to what degree a communicative approach should be adopted. Will students internalise the grammar of the target language without any form of explicit grammar focus, or will this lead to early fossilisation as has been suggested? Should the teacher follow the exhortations of Krashen, Terrell and the like, or try for some sort of integration.

Yalden (1983), advocates what she calls a 'proportional approach' to communicative syllabus design, in which, as a learner progresses, the proportion of grammatical input is gradually decreased and the proportion of functional input is gradually increased. The approach is represented in the following diagram. Beginners (at Point I) spend about eighty per cent of the time mastering the rudiments of the grammatical system, and move eventually through to an advanced level (III) where only about twenty per cent of the class time is devoted to grammar and eighty percent is devoted to communicative function. Interestingly, in Australia at present, the proportions seem to work the other way, there being a functional orientation with beginners and a grammatical focus with more advanced students.

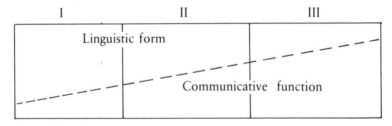

Figure 4: The Proportional Approach (Yalden, 1983: 122)

6 Content Considerations

Most of this discussion has been centred on the selection of formal and functional input and the principles for its gradation. However, these are by no means the only principles upon which syllabuses can be based. Others include situational, topical and thematic principles. These pose the same problems for syllabus designers as all non-grammatical criteria, namely those related to establishing the guiding principles for selecting and sequencing input.

Whatever the basis for input selection, a central problem remains the selection of interesting experiential content in which to clothe the structures, functions and so on. Selecting interesting and relevant content is a difficult task, and one which seems to have received little attention in the literature. One of the problems in developing general courses for adults is that the range of interests of the learners in a given group will be quite diverse. What is interesting to one learner is not necessarily going to be interesting to another.

It is through needs analysis and negotiated goal setting that this problem can be overcome.

A partial solution to the problem has been sought in the development of special purpose courses (although this has led to all sorts of other unanticipated problems). In schools there has been a move towards language courses based on the subjects of the school curriculum. For general English courses, however, the problem remains.

From an inspection of published materials, it would seem that most course and materials writers proceed on an intuitive basis when selecting content. In general EFL materials similar topics and themes occur time and again. More often than not, these include:

Famous people and events
Entertainment

Newspapers—reports, advertisements etc.
Accidents and curious incidents
Making and doing things
The environment

The following list of topics from a recently published course-book illustrates the 'scattergun' approach adopted by course designers who have no clear idea of the interests of their target clientele:

Summer holidays in England
Wedding invitations
Bob Dylan
Bus and train timetables
Describing a house
Camera operating instructions
The Olympic Games
Stamp dispensing machines
Ernest Hemingway
Recipe—making hamburgers
Appollo moon landing
Cassette player—how to use
Comparing cars
Job advertisements
Motorcycles
Road accident report
The story of tea

Content selection for courses designed for migrants and refugees is in many ways easier than for foreign language students. The former, despite varied backgrounds, do at least have the common experience of being new-comers to the country, and a needs analysis should reveal suitable content areas for the course designer.

In practice, however, things are not quite so straightforward. Despite their common experiences, different interests and degrees of interest are brought into the classroom by the learner, and these have an effect on what goes on there. As a simple example, most teachers are aware of the difficulty of interesting middle-aged (and often not so middle-aged) men in topics connected with shopping and food.

One possible solution to the problem of providing interesting and relevant content in situations where specific purpose courses are inappropriate, is to group students according to criteria other than language proficiency. At present, the overwhelming majority of students in the AMEP are assigned to a class on the basis of their ASLPR rating, and such students often share very little apart from the proficiency rating level at the time of being interviewed for placement.

Other criteria for grouping students which might allow teachers to select more relevant content include age, sex, educational background, nationality, level of literacy, occupational background and length of time in Australia. Of course, having greater heterogeneity of language proficiency creates other problems, and it would be up to the teacher to decide whether these additional problems are outweighed by the advantages of embracing alternative grouping procedures. In larger centres several teachers working with students at the same level could possibly regroup students and still have homogeneous classes.

7   Ordering Input

The traditional method of ordering input was in terms of linguistic notions of simplicity and complexity. Those items considered to be linguistically simple were taught before those which were considered to be complex. Thus, the simple present tense was taught before the simple past because it was considered to be simpler. These items were then generally organised into a linear format which the learner moved systematically through, learning one discrete feature at a time. This discrete linear approach seemed like good sense from a pedogogical point of view; the learner worked from the simple to the difficult and was only expected to learn one thing at a time.

While some language teachers have consistently advocated non-linear teaching, (Newmark, for example, was for years a voice crying in the wilderness), the discrete point linear approach was the norm until quite recently. It is really only since the development of communicative language teaching that a non-linear approach to the design and development of language teaching syllabuses have gained any sort of widespread support.

The rising popularity of non-linear approaches has by no means meant the death of linear approaches. In fact, linear courses have surfaced in their most fully articulated form in recent years in the direct instruction (DI) movement. This natural child of programmed instruction has, not surprisingly, been particularly influential in the United States where it has underpinned the development of the Distar language program.

The spectacular results claimed for DI may well owe as much to the learning environment (usually intensive one-to-one with carefully and professionally produced materials) as to the DI syllabus design procedure itself. Again, test results may be more a reflection of the test (discrete point language items) than of communicative ability on the part of the learner.

The linear—non-linear distinction parallels in many ways the distinction drawn by Wilkins (1976), between synthetic and analytic approaches to language teaching. Wilkins designates as synthetic those approaches which break the language down into discrete components for presentation to the learner, and in which the final task for the learner is to reassemble those components in productive language use.

In analytic approaches, the learner is confronted with chunks of natural language and is required to extract from these the necessary linguistic generalisations. In Wilkins' work, grammatical approaches are naturally associated with synthetic syllabuses, while notional approaches are associated with analytic ones.

Although it is possible to have linear programs with an implicit methodology and non-linear programs in which there is some explicit teaching, non-linear programs would normally be associated with an implicit approach to the development within the learner of the appropriate linguistic generalisations. In other words, learners would be left to intuit the regularities of the language through exposure to natural language data, and communicative tasks derived from these rather than having these regularities (or rules) explicitly taught.

Those who advocate an implicit approach within a non-linear framework usually do so on the grounds that rules are too complex and contain too many exceptions to be explicitly taught in a way that would enable them to be used by the learner in the process of communicating, and that in any case, the process of utilisation is too laborious for them to be useful in communicative language use. Another observation is that the end result of using conscious rules is not always accurate or fluent language use.

One person with a long-standing interest in the issue of linear versus non-linear language programs is Winitz (1981). Although a great deal of his work is concerned with language-retarded first-language users, many of the points he makes about developmental language acquisition are also applicable to second language learners.

One of his major points is that correct usage is not an all-or-nothing matter, that the appearance of a given item represents the end point of a complex learning process. He illustrates this with an example taken from child syntactic development:

> When children first demonstrate use of the progressive, for the most part in the present tense, the auxiliary is often omitted. An example is, 'The dog

barking' for 'The dog is barking'. One explanation for the omission of the auxiliary is that it is not a salient unit of expression for the child (Brown and Fraser, 1964; Winitz and Reeds, 1975). Young children can understand the essential 'meaning' of the progressive by the -ing marker, and by the environmental and linguistic context. The auxiliary is initially not critical for the understanding of simple progressive expressions. (Winitz, 1981: 3)

The auxiliary becomes salient when later structures, for example, passives and question formation are learned. Winitz goes on to say that:

It can be argued that until 'is' correctly appears in progressives, the present progressive, as a syntactic construction, has not been acquired. Certain conceptual aspects of the progressive have, no doubt, been acquired, but the various forms of the progressive, as well as the difference between the progressive and other grammatical structures, may not yet be completely learned. Possibly, full understanding of the progressive cannot come about until late developing structures (present progressive versus question, or present progressive versus truncated relative clause, for example) are acquired. If our reasoning is correct, the development of language may involve linguistic knowledge acquired from experience with linguistic stages of varying complexity. (p.4)

One implication of Winitz's analysis is that, while a given language stage indicates a particular level of linguistic knowledge, it does not give any indication of the sequencing whereby this knowledge was obtained. It also assumes a one-to-one correspondence between comprehension and production. In Winitz's non-linear model, no such assumptions are made. It is accepted that structures may be comprehended which are well in advance of oral production, and that linguistic experiences at more advanced levels may assist in the internalisation of structures first encountered at earlier stages.

Winitz cites Lahey and Bloom (1977), as advocates of indirect teaching within a linear framework. The example provided concerns the acquisition of pronominalisation. The clinician uses such forms without drawing attention to them in any explicit manner when teaching lexical items, and then observes production by the child to see whether the given item appears. Winitz points out that if some forms can be learned through this casual presentation, then it should be possible for all the morphological and syntactic aspects of the language to be so taught.

A major problem of indirect non-linear teaching at an elementary level is that the learner may be so overwhelmed by the flood of incomprehensible language to which he/she is exposed that he/she may switch off altogether. Newmark (1981), has pointed out that the crucial factor in successful second language acquisition is that the learner must be attending to the language while experiencing its meaning. He suggests that perhaps the central characteristic distinguishing good from poor teachers is their ability to command attention, and that good and poor students may likewise be differentiated by their ability to pay attention.

Strevens (1984), has pointed out that a linear approach fails to take account of the fact that intake flow consists of streams of segments, each of which has multiple meanings, and that parts of these multiple meanings are learned simultaneously during repeated exposure to segments. Learning is a process in which the learner gradually increases his/her grasp of target items and as nucleation occurs does so faster, with greater precision and with a wider range of meanings and implications. In short, 'learning is not a sequence of single shot learnings of single presentations of discrete, mono-semantic items'.

A number of experiments have been conducted with what may be called 'semantic syllabuses'. In these, no attempt is made to systematically sequence grammatical input in the early stages of learning. Rather, the teacher concentrates on building up an extensive vocabulary in the learner. The theory behind the approach is similar to that espoused by Krashen, that by 'going for meaning' the learner will automatically acquire structure, and that language development is a matter of moving from meaning to form rather than the other way round. The advantage of the approach is that it obviates the need to sequence, cluster or stage grammatical input. The disadvantage is that it may simply be wrong, and that students exposed to this approach may never, in fact, acquire structure. Given the enormous difficulties of controlling variables, the issue will probably never be settled empirically. Whether vocabulary based courses ever achieve widespread popularity will probably depend on whether teachers themselves feel they are worthwhile.

Two experiments in vocabulary based courses are reported in Nunan (1983) and Terrell (1982).

The course reported in Nunan (1983), was developed for low level low ability learners who had experienced difficulty with structural/functional courses. Some idea of the way the course was structured can be gained from the following quotation:

> As semantic rather than formal criteria were involved in formulating this project, the selection of input on grammatical grounds was largely avoided . . . As the students were at a low level, much early input was based on common semantic fields. In the first month of the course, for instance, the following areas were covered: identification of self and others; common actions; talking about self and others; household objects; colours; parts of the body; visiting the doctor; shopping and food . . . While the emphasis was on communicating meanings (rather than drilling sets of predetermined structures) a great deal of structural repetition occurred naturally as a function of the activities used. In fact, learners covered most of the grammatical forms encountered in structural syllabuses (pp.4-5).
>
> This view (that vocabulary should be limited in order to allow the learner to master structure) is widespread in language teaching circles (see, for example, Gattegno, 1972) and is based on the notion that fluency and understanding develop through the learning structures and the practice of these structures in communication. The view adopted here is just the opposite, that in both first and second language development, meaning is acquired first . . . and that is used as the basis for the acquisition of structure . . . language teaching ought to be based on the development of relevant semantic networks rather than syntactic structures. (p.10)

In the same vein, Terrell (1982), criticises the view that vocabulary development is the least important aspect of second or foreign language learning. He points out that, in fact, if students have a large enough vocabulary, they will be able to comprehend and speak a great deal of the target language, even though their master of the structures of the language is minimal.

The major issue raised in this section concerns the degree to which a linear, discrete point, as opposed to a non-linear approach to the grading of input is adopted. Added to these is a methodological dimension relating to the degree to which pedagogical points are explicitly taught or implicitly introduced. Although it is possible to place these on a scale, with explicit, linear, formal teaching at one end, and implicit, non-linear, functional teaching at the other, this is misleading. Although it is more likely for a structural course to be linear in its organisation and explicit in its methodology, and for a functional course to be non-linear and implicit, than the other way round, there is no necessary reason for these variables to be automatically aligned in this way. It is possible to have any combination of these (although some combinations are much less likely than others). The variables can best be represented on a three dimensional scale.

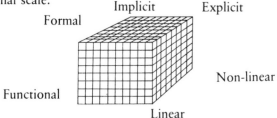

Figure 5: Input Variables in Syllabus Design

It has already been mentioned that, given the difficulties inherent in conducting empirical research, it is unlikely that we are going to get definitive answers to the central problems of input selection and gradation in the near future, if ever. It is possible, however, to come to some tentative conclusions which may serve as a practical guide to syllabus, materials and methodological development. The first of these is that coherent programs will only result from an integrated consideration of syllabus, materials and methodological issues, rather than keeping them divorced as has tended to happen in the past. Second, given the complexity of the task and the fact that learner variables will be crucial in determining the success or otherwise of a teaching program, the ultimate decisions about what gets taught when and how must rest with the teacher. The days when 'teacher-proof' packages were seen as the solution to problems inherent in the classroom are hopefully long gone. What teachers need are materials and techniques which reflect current views on the nature of language and language learning which can be integrated into current programs or used as a basis for the development of new programs and courses.

Given the fact that materials exist for teachers inclined towards a traditional view of language learning and teaching, new materials and content suggestions should reflect some of the current ideas discussed in this section. That is, they should have a communicative focus, should be capable of a non-linear exploitation and should allow for implicit forms of exploitation. These themes are returned to and given greater substance in later sections after consideration has been given to other issues such as the development and exploitation of authentic materials.

8 Linguistic Staging

A growing awareness of the deficiencies of a strictly sequential, grammar based approach to language design led to the development of what Wilkins (1976), terms 'analytic' approaches to design and methodology. Here, the learner is presented with chunks of the target language and is required to draw out significant linguistic generalisations.

Most approaches growing out of the so-called acquisition model (Krashen, 1981; Nunan, 1983: Krashen and Terrell, 1983) are basically analytic, requiring the learner to cope with chunks of language containing grammatical structures which have not been pre-taught. The learner comprehends by mapping the non-verbal clues provided by the teacher onto the language input. These approaches pose particular problems for certain types of learners, in particular adult beginners and what might be termed the slow learner. Most adults want some sort of systematic exposure to the language in the early stages and are less prepared than children to tolerate large quantities of incomprehensible input.

One solution for teachers wishing to provide more realistic non-linear linguistic models on the one hand, and yet to limit input on the other, is to use a staging approach. Such an approach departs from a linear, grammatical one in both input and methodology. From the beginning, learners are exposed to chunks of language which approximate to normal discourse, and in which functional and notional, as well as linguistic criteria are taken into consideration. Unlike a total analytical approach, however, input at each stage is controlled to some degree.

GRAMMAR	FUNCTIONS	NOTIONS	TOPICS
Verb 'be'	Identifying	Identification	Self and others
Demonstratives	Naming	Colour	Shopping
Pronouns	Describing	Size	The body
Possessive adjective	Entities/actions	Proximity	About the house
Predicative adjectives	Locating entities/ actions	Nationality	Getting around
Who - questions	Requesting	Age	
Who, what were		Actions	
Simple present			
Prepositions of place			

GENERAL OBJECTIVES

—identifies common objects in the experiential world
—describes gross features of objects and entities
—identifies self
—understands and responds to requests for personal details
—requests goods in familiar shopping contexts
—requests basic information

Figure 6: Sample Content Frame for a Staging Syllabus

Frames such as the one above are used as a guide in the development of units, modules and individual lessons for learners working at a given stage. They provide guidance in the selection of the linguistic features appropriate for focused activities at a given stage, for the selection or production of texts for input and also for appropriate exploitation activities.

9   Acquisition Research

It should be obvious from the foregoing sections that there is currently a great deal of confusion and uncertainty surrounding the development of language syllabuses, particularly in the selection and ordering of input. However, there are indications that recent research into second language acquisition may be able to provide us with pedagogically and psycholinguistically sound principles for selecting and ordering our syllabuses.

As has already been pointed out, linguistically ordered syllabuses fell into disfavour because they did not work very efficiently. There was a mismatch between what was taught and what was learned. Dissatisfaction with grammatical syllabuses led to the development of functional/notional syllabuses, in which grammatical features of the language were given less prominence than hitherto. The assumption was that linguistic grading led to syllabuses in which the language was decontextualised and unnatural, and that the task confronting the learner, of having to reintegrate the decomposed bits of language into a coherent whole, created unnecessary problems when it came to using the language communicatively.

Results of language acquisition research which has recently become available, however, suggest additional reasons for the unsatisfactory nature of linguistically sequenced syllabuses. The most comprehensive piece of research in the acquisition of English as a second language is that by Johnston (1984, 1985). This work has great potential significance for language syllabus design and materials development.

Johnston's research is far too detailed to be described in any detail here. The interested reader is referred to the original research report or the detailed description of the project listed in the references. Basically, Johnston studied the order in which second language learners acquire certain syntactic and morphological features of English. He discovered that certain linguistic items are acquired in a fixed order, an order which can be accounted for in terms of a psycholinguistic model derived from work in speech processing. What Johnston discovered was that there are marked disparities between the natural order in which learners acquire features and the order in which they are presented and taught in published syllabuses and coursebooks.

After analysing the grading order of two widely used coursebooks, Johnston has this to say:

> It should now be clear that pedagogic grading and 'natural' grading are radically divergent and even contradictory.
>
> Equally, pedagogical notions about learning processes and the psychological organisation of learning are strongly at variance with what can be inferred from empirical studies. (Johnston, 1984:390)

He goes on to suggest that, if syllabuses and materials are organised according to acquisitional sequences, formal learning can have a facilitating effect on language development.

As a result of Johnston's research, it now seems clear that

i. formal learning and error correction can have a facilitating effect if the language items being worked on are appropriate to the learner's stage of development;

ii. attempting to teach items which are beyond the learner's current stage of development can have an inhibiting and detrimental effect;

iii. presenting language as disembodied paradigms is detrimental;

iv. ignoring learning principles such as elaboration by discrimination (in which learning proceeds through the elaboration of a simple set of optimal distinctions) is detrimental.

While the bulk of Johnston's research is still relatively inaccessible to the classroom teacher, there are a number of immediate implications of his work. Even without knowing the details of his research, it is possible to take account of general principles such as those outlined above in program planning. In particular:

i. present language in context;

ii. concentrate on developing receptive competence, particularly in the early stages;

iii. emphasise meaningful language use rather than the manipulation of forms;

iv. do not insist on the use of grammatical forms beyond the learner's given stage of competence (sensitive monitoring of student output should indicate whether a learner is ready for a given structure);

v. teach one thing at a time (e.g. do not introduce more than one use of a given structure at a time).

(These particular points reflect my own interpretation of Johnson's research, and not all of them will necessarily be subscribed to by Johnson himself. They reiterate or echo points made in other sections of this work.)

10 Materials

Without doubt, the most significant move in the area of materials has been towards the use of authentic sources in the classroom. 'Authenticity' has in fact become a bit of a catchword, and like many catchwords tends to be accepted without criticism or analysis.

'Authentic' materials are usually defined as those which have been produced for purposes other than to teach language. They can be culled from many different sources: video clips, recordings of authentic interactions, extracts from television, radio and newspapers, signs, maps and charts, photographs and pictures, timetables and schedules. These are just a few of the sources which have been tapped.

Teachers who attempt to use authentic materials in the classroom encounter many problems. Perhaps the first of these is collecting the material in the first place. While obtaining printed material might be relatively straightforward, it is much more difficult to obtain authentic samples of aural language. The very act of recording the source can very often destroy its authenticity. Another problem is that of coverage. To what extent are the materials seen to represent the total language system, and to what extent are they seen as a sample? How representative is the sample? If key language structures and functions do not occur in the samples, are these items omitted from one's syllabus? If not, is one forced to 'contrive' authentic materials which contain them? How does one develop interesting coherent units of work from authentic materials which are pedestrian and piecemeal? These are all questions which need to be addressed by teachers wanting to use authentic materials. The problem of finding solutions and answers has often forced teachers to develop 'realistic' or 'authentic-like' materials.

Whilst most teachers would accept the value of using authentic materials with advanced learners at least some, if not all of the time, the use of authentic materials with beginners has been questioned. This raises the question of whether the use of such materials is an immediate or an ultimate objective. If it is seen as an ultimate objective, then there is no reason why non-authentic materials could not be used providing they were written with the specific objective of taking the learner towards the goal of comprehending authentic materials. Accepting the validity of using non-authentic materials at certain stages and levels does not mean that one is constrained to using totally artificial and unrealistic dialogues and texts. The following tape transcript is from a non-authentic source (non-authentic in that it is part of a non-scripted monologue produced for the purposes of language teaching). It is, however, infinitely more realistic than most specially written dialogues and texts.

> I generally do my fruit and veg. shopping on Saturday morning—you know—sort of, er, early, like. Not too many people around, kind of thing. Usually buy the same stuff every week, oh . . . First up, the heavy stuff, you know, potatoes—potatoes and, er, onions, yeah onions. Oh, carrots, too. Always buy carrots. Usually get a, what you call, a cabbage, too, if it's not too expensive. Fruit? Well, now, let's see. Apples, yeah. And b . . .bananas. We all like them. What else?

Brown and Yule (1983), address ways of teaching oral language skills using an approach based on the analysis of conversational English. They identify boredom as a problem in the use of authentic spontaneous conversations, pointing out that:

> It is the participation in conversations which makes us such avid talkers,. the 'need to know' or the 'need to tell' or the 'need to be friendly'. You can listen to hours and hours of recorded conversation without finding anything that interests you from the point of view of what the speakers are talking about or what they are saying about it. After all, their conversation was not intended for the overhearer. It was intended for them as participants. This is often hard for course constructors to realise. (p.82)

While there are topics such as death, sex and danger which have widespread appeal, it is hardly feasible to construct a complete course on these. Given the difficulties involved in finding universally interesting materials, Brown and Yule suggest that:

> The emphasis should be moved from attempting to provide intrinsically interesting materials, which we have just claimed is generally impossible, to doing interesting things with materials . . . these materials should be chosen, not so much on the basis of their own interest, as for what they can be used to do. (p.83)

The emphasis thus moves from the materials themselves to the sorts of ways in which these might be exploited.

Despite the difficulties associated with using authentic sources, Brown and Yule insist on the use of what they call 'naturally occurring' conversations as source texts rather than scripted dialogues. This is because scripted dialogues are invariably artificial. Even those that appear naturalist are quite different from genuine instances of language use. The problem, as Belasco (1981) and others have pointed out, is that comprehending and manipulating scripted dialogues does not readily transfer to comprehending and using language in real communicative situations.

Despite the difficulties, it is imperative that future materials development projects be biased towards the use of authentic or 'realistic' sources. The advantages of using such sources have been documented. If our intention is to assist learners to exploit the language learning potential in the environment (which is a key AMEP objective) then the introduction of authentic sources into the classroom should be the aim of every teacher.

To repeat, however, this does not mean that teachers must work exclusively or even principally with authentic materials from the very beginning. The ability of learners to exploit such materials is an aim to be worked towards.

11 Activities

For many teachers, the most difficult and time consuming task confronting them is the development of activities to exploit the materials they have collected or created. It is also something which preoccupies teachers, who see the setting of classroom tasks as methodological. Unfortunately, in many cases learning activities are developed in an uncoordinated and isolated fashion. In other words, they are not interrelated with other elements of syllabus design. This a carryover from the days when teachers were not seen as having a role to play in most other aspects of syllabus development. It is also partly a reflection of the fact that teachers are under tremendous pressure and simply do not have time to spend on developing an integrated view of syllabus design and methodology.

The move towards the use of authentic materials has obviously had an important effect on the types of activities and tasks which students are set. In particular the notion of difficulty has had to be reconsidered. Instead of producing materials in which the language is simplified to reflect the ability level of the learner, the use of authentic source texts necessitates the development of activities at different levels of difficulty. In other words, it is not the text itself, but what the student is expected to do with the text which is regulated. Such an approach has the advantage that a given text can be used with a wide range of learners, and is thus particularly amenable to mixed ability groups and community classes. A disadvantage is the tendency for learners at all levels to want to understand at once the totality of the input with which they are working. Until they are taught otherwise, there is a tendency, for instance, for learners to want to understand every word in a dialogue or written text. In the previous section the transcript of a short monologue is presented. While this contains language which is beyond the capabilities of the beginning learner, it is not difficult to think of activities which would be appropriate for learners at this level. One could, for instance, get them to identify the items of food which are named by pointing these out on a chart or separating pictures of named items from those that do not occur in the monologue. One could get the learner to make repeated passes through the text, processing it at increasingly complex levels. Here, complexity is cognitive rather than grammatical.

There is almost no limit to the number of activities which can be devised to exploit materials at different levels of difficulty. The figure below shows one way of representing these. As one moves from the top of the typology to the bottom, the cognitive and performance demands made on the learner becomes greater. At the top, the learner processes the source and is not required to respond overtly in any way. At the bottom, the learner is required to engage in problem solving tasks and discussions and become involved in negotiating meaning.

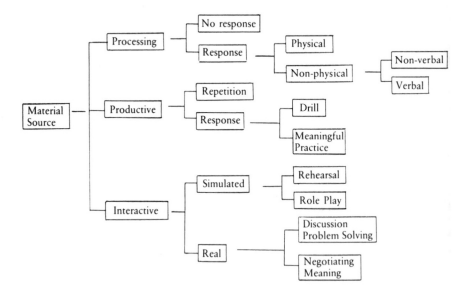

Figure 7: A Typology of Activities Graded According to Cognitive Complexity

Proponents of authenticity such as Candlin and Edelhoff (1982), insist that not only should materials be authentic, but activities and tasks should be authentic as well. In other words, the tasks derived from a given source ought to reflect the purposes beyond language learning for which the text itself was originally produced. This is a fairly obvious and straightforward principle to follow when the source itself suggests the task, as for example, in the case of maps and timetables, or texts describing entities and processes. However, not all textual sources are as amenable to exploitation as maps and timetables, and it is not always possible to derive tasks that could conceivably be carried out for 'authentic' purposes.

While it may or may not be the case that language is best acquired when carrying out tasks where the focus is not on the language, as Krashen and Terrell (1983) suggest, the simple fact is that students enter language classes, and take part in the tasks and activities set for them with the express purpose of learning/acquiring the target language. No matter how absorbing the task of assembling the clues required for solving a problem or completing a jigsaw learning task, the learner has gone to the effort of coming to class, not to solve problems, but to learn a language. To that extent, it is difficult to make statements about task authenticity. All tasks and activities will be more or less non-authentic.

In their introduction to the *Challenges* course, Candlin and Edelhoff (1982), state that:

> It is not enough, however, simply to present learners with a range of connected text-types if they are asked to perform fundamentally inauthentic tasks with the texts. One doesn't read a bus ticket or a train time-table in order to learn something about English grammar; you read them to check if the bus conductor has sold you the correct ticket. (p.9)

The fact is, however, that in the classroom the learner's primary purpose in processing data is, in fact, to learn English. He/she is basically not interested in whether 'the 9.15 to Lancaster really makes you change at Preston'.

When, in fact, one analyses the tasks, exercises and activities on which the course, *Challenges*, is based one finds that few of these can be said to fulfil the task authenticity criterion; most, in fact, are rather traditional. For example:

1. Matching:
   Make true sentences about Irwin, Phil and Steve (students are required to match the two halves of a sentence).
2. Listening and Note-taking
   Listen to the girl talking about the job she wants when she leaves school. Note what she says about her job under the headings above the picture.
3. Tell your group about the job you would like and its advantages and disadvantages. This (substitution) table will help you.
4. Open drill: Making suggestions,
   (Listen to the tape). Introduce and make your own suggestions:
   Girl: Now let's think about new things for the club room. Has anyone got any ideas what to buy?
   . . . .
   Boy: I've got a great idea what to buy.
   Girl: Tell us then.
   . . . .
   Girl: What do you think Gabby?

While these activities may serve useful and valid language learning purposes, by no stretch of the imagination could they be said to be authentic in the sense that they are tasks which are likely to be carried out by someone not engaged in language learning.

There is another sense in which Candlin and Edelhoff use the term 'task authenticity'. This is when learners' responses reflect their own particular feelings, attitudes and opinions. They say that:

> any act of reading or listening is itself a piece of authentic communication in which our ideas and experiences interact with those of the speaker or author. Some texts, of course, are designed to admit only one interpretation (say warnings or instructions) but many other texts . . . offer many different interpretations. Readers and learners need to be able to work authentically at these texts, teasing out and constructing their own meanings. The authenticity of this kind of learner task derives from the essential authenticity of any individual response. (p.9)

It is clear from this quote that its authors are, in fact, referring more to the authenticity of response than the authenticity of the task. Thus, while answering comprehension questions is not, of itself, a typically authentic task, the responses of the learning may be more or less authentic to the extent to which they reflect the learner's real attitudes, preferences and beliefs.

One principle which lends coherence to what are often a rather disparate series of activities is the task-dependency principle (Johnson, 1982; Candlin and Edelhoff, 1982). Using this technique, the materials writer decides on a terminal task which is authentic to the point of taking the learner beyond the language itself to the performance of the specified tasks. All the activities leading up to the task itself should provide the learner with all the requisite skills necessary for the task to be carried out. Corbel (1984), has utilised this principle and integrated it with the notion of action sequences to derive a procedure for course and materials design.

12 Mode and Environment

Learning mode refers to whether the learner is operating on an individual or group basis. If operating on an individual basis, is the learner self-paced but teacher directed or self-directed? If the learner is operating as part of a group, is the group for mostly whole class, small group or pair work? Each of the modes has implications for syllabus and materials design.

It is comparatively rare for the learner to be operating totally in one mode to the exclusion of all others. This is particularly so for group modes where, typically, there is a mixture of whole group, small group, pair work and some teacher-directed individualisation. It is up to the teacher to decide which mode is most suitable for the course objectives at any given stage, and to organise the learners accordingly.

With the development of self-access centres, a great deal of interest has been generated in individualised modes. This interest has been fostered by the greater flexibility offered within the Program by the availability of self-access centres. Properly organised and staffed centres would allow increased options, and more flexible learning arrangements. Such flexibility is desirable given the range and diversity of learners within the Program.

At present, there are two major and interrelated problems with self-access centres. The first of these is conceptual, the second largely practical. The conceptual problem concerns the nature of key concepts such as self-access, self-direction and individualisation. While there are similarities between these concepts, there are also differences. It is important that these differences be sorted out. Probably the key concept, and certainly the most contentious one, is that of student-directed learning. Here it is the student rather than the teacher who decides what should be learned and, to a certain extent, how learning should proceed.

The second essentially practical problem concerns the lack of suitable materials for self-access and individualised modes of learning. The bulk of materials in most centres has been derived from classroom based sources. Some of this is adapted, although more often it has merely been adopted. There is not necessarily anything wrong with such materials; however, they do not represent the full range of options available. This gap in materials probably reflects the lack of clarity about the nature of self-access learning.

While the early impetus towards individualisation was derived from behaviourist-based programmed instruction, the development of communicative language teaching has provided a more contemporary rationale for this particular mode. If it is accepted that learners differ in the rates at which they learn and the types of learning strategies which suit them best, and if learning to communicate involves actual practice in communicating (something which is not necessarily given), then alternative strategies have to be devised to the teachers-versus-students model of classroom organisation. While there are times when the teacher will address the whole class, there also needs to be provision for learners to work in pairs, in small groups and on their own, as well as opportunities for interacting with native speakers.

It may seem paradoxical to talk in terms of individualisation within the communicative classroom. However, there are components of the language which may be most effectively mastered by the learner working alone with the supervision and assistance of the teacher. This holds, not only for reading and writing, but for pronunciation, listening comprehension and vocabulary development. For beginning students, the development of a core vocabulary is one of the most important, if not the most important task; a fact recognised by learners, if not by teachers. The ability to learn vocabulary is one in which learners differ quite markedly, some being able to internalise core vocabulary without too much apparent effort, and others needing to spend a great deal of time and effort on the task. Learning vocabulary is one area where an individualised approach may be the best one to adopt. Using a cassette recorder integrated with a microprocessor and in association with visuals, beginners, even illiterates, can work on their own in developing a core functional vocabulary. They can spend as much time as they wish, independent of the teacher, working through the materials. The hardware can be programmed so that the learner is unable to proceed until mastery is demonstrated at each stage.

A number of researchers have voiced the belief that first language development occurs largely as a function of genuine one-to-one interactions (see, for example, Wells, 1981). If it is accepted that it is of value for second language learners also to engage in such interactions, perhaps we ought to try and build these into our programs. While it is, of course, impossible in the classroom to provide a native speaking peer tutor for each language learner, there are a number of ways in which one-to-one contact might be increased. An important first step is to accept the value to the learner, even the low-level learner, of engaging in genuine interactions (that is, interactions in which the intention is to negotiate meanings rather than to manipulate forms). One technique is to have an extended one-to-one or small group dialogue, negotiating meanings with some sort of input stimulus. Another is to arrange the teaching timetable so there is time for a fifteen minute one-to-one consultation with each student every week. Such an arrangement means that work will have to be arranged for the rest of the class during the time scheduled for the individual consultations. With twenty students in a group, this would amount to five hours a week. However, teachers who have tried such an arrangement generally feel it is well worthwhile, particularly if it is carried out in conjunction with self-access centres.

Greater flexibility can also be achieved if several teachers working with roughly similar ability levels are able to collaborate in some form of team teaching. If the students are all working on a similar program, it should be possible to arrange things so that for varying periods students have the opportunity of working intensively on a one-to-one basis while the rest of the group (up to, say, sixty) is being supervised by one of the teachers. Belasco (1981), provides an example of how one team teaching arrangement was used to achieve mastery learning by a group of foreign language students. The system involved a team of five teachers working with 125 students. To begin with, each teacher had 25 students. Those who achieved 90 per cent advanced to the next unit, while the others repeated the first unit with one or two teachers. After 30 weeks, there were students in all ten units of the program with each of the five teachers having responsibility for two of the units. In commenting on the system, Belasco says:

... no one enters the second year of foreign language training until he or she has achieved 90 per cent or better in the first year ... the student advances at a pace set by his or her own capacity. (p.32)

Alternative teaching/learning modes other than self-access have been available within the AMEP for some time. These include the Home Tutor Scheme and the Correspondence Course. It is probably time that the pedagogical and organisational bases of these courses are evaluated. Questions for those administering the Home Tutor Scheme include the following:

How does the HTS relate to the other services available?

Would it be possible to reorganise the Scheme so that it would be more effectively articulated with other learning provisions?

What is the pedagogical and social role of tutors?

What sort of training provisions should be made for tutors?

What sort of materials should be developed to support the Scheme?

The Correspondence Course is currently being phased out, and the new Distance Learning Course should be available for use early in 1986. This course is the result of a fairly radical re-evaluation of language teaching pedagogy, and incorporates a number of the ideas already discussed in this paper. The two most significant of these are the use of authentic source materials and the incorporation of 'learning how to learn' aims and objectives into the design of the course. These include the following:

1. To help learners to become aware of their own learning strategies and to build on and apply these to the specific task of language learning.

2. To alert learners to the possibilities for continual English language learning within their total linguistic environment.

3. To promote learners' confidence in their own ability to learn language both within and outside the confines of a structured course (Gray and Kleist, 1983: 2).

Objectives such as these should be promoted throughout the AMEP, and it is to be hoped that the Distance Learning Course will provide a model to all teachers, not just those teaching through a distance mode.

The learning environment, which is closely connected to mode, refers to where the learning takes place. Until comparatively recently, it was assumed that learning would take place within the four walls of the classroom. With the recognition that a primary task for the language teacher is to assist the learner utilise the language being learned for purposes beyond the classroom, that assumption is being challenged. More and more courses, in whole or in part, are being conducted in environments where the learner is going to be hearing and using English. The Courses in Industry programs are well known. In addition, language learning classes are being organised in institutions such as hospitals and schools. One of the most successful of these courses has been the Language of Childbirth program (Diesendorf, Lockwood and Perkins, 1984). In 1985 a team of teachers in South Australia is to conduct a program aimed at monitoring, coordinating and expanding community based learning experiences for their students. The aim of this program is to teach students how to make the most of real experiences to learn the English that is relevant to their lives. It is important that these initiatives be encouraged through program innovation, and that their results be disseminated.

13 Evaluation

Evaluation is an area of curriculum development and syllabus design which has caused problems in all areas of education. The first question to be asked is what is being evaluated? Is it the learner, the teacher, the materials, the methods, or is it the entire learning environment which includes all of these? In recent years people involved in evaluation have concerned themselves with more than simply testing learning rates among students, although this is probably still the single most important aspect of evaluation. During the seventies, an alternative to the psychometric approach to evaluation was developed. This became known as the 'anthropological paradigm' because of the similarity between methods used by the evaluator and those of the anthropologist. Here, the evaluator attempts to enter the bloodstream of the educational institution and obtain a portrait of the learning endeavour using case study techniques, diaries and so on, as well as the more traditional tools of questionnaires and psychometric assessment.

The ultimate rationale of any teaching program is that, at the end of the program, the learner should, as a result of that program, be a different person than he/she was at the beginning. This difference may manifest itself in different ways; in terms of knowledge gained, skills acquired, attitude changes and so on. In considering ways of determining whether changes have taken place and measuring the amount of change, the evaluator has to consider many different questions. These will include the following:

> What form of assessment would be most appropriate?
> Do any tests which are developed measure what the course purported to teach?
> Will the same results obtain if the same learners are tested on different occasions?
> Will the same results be obtained from different markers?

Does the test cover a representative sample of items from the syllabus?

Is it appropriate to attempt to evaluate unintended learning outcomes?

To what extent are the testing and evaluation procedures influencing what goes on in the classroom? Is this influence healthy or not?

Over the years there have been many different types of language tests developed for a variety of purposes. The most influential of these such as TOEFL in the United States and the Cambridge examinations in England were principally designed for students intending to undertake courses of study at tertiary institutions in which English is the medium of instruction. These tests tend to be 'traditional' in the sense that they consist largely of tests of discrete point grammatical items along with various sorts of tests of reading and aural comprehension. Changes to the format of the tests, such as supplementing multiple choice tests with cloze tests, have hardly been radical.

With the development of communicative language teaching, it was felt that tests ought to be developed which reflected the new ideas. In other words, testers were not satisfied that traditional tests measured the communicative abilities which the newer syllabuses were purporting to teach.

In Britain, the Royal Society of Arts has taken a lead in developing communicative language tests. In 1981, it introduced an examination in the 'Communicative Use of English as a Foreign Language', and in 1984 it ran a pilot project aimed at developing a Certificate in English as a Second Language.

The development of the test of the Communicative Use of English as a Foreign Language was a conscious attempt to develop new testing procedures to reflect developments in communicative language teaching. The test is principally aimed at foreign language learners in Britain and abroad, although an ESL option is also included. The Examination itself has seven principal characteristics. These are as follows:

1. The tests are operational, that is, they are intended to measure what learners can do in English.
2. The tests have claims to authenticity in terms of the tasks which the learners are asked to perform and the texts which they are expected to process and produce.

Tasks and texts thus purport to be the same as those confronting native speakers.

3. The examinations are intended for candidates who are living, working or studying in Britain or who intend visiting the country on a long or short-term basis.
4. The examination is offered at basic, intermediate and advanced levels.
5. At each level, four independent tests are offered. These are listening, reading, writing and oral interaction.
6. Candidates may enter for any combination of tests at any combination of levels.
7. The content of the examinations is taken from the following areas, which are meant to reflect the general areas in which candidates will want to use English:
   — Social interaction with native and non-native speakers of English.
   — Dealing with official and semi-official bodies.
   — Shopping and using services.
   — Visiting places of interest and entertainment.
   — Travelling and arranging for travel.
   — Using media for information and entertainment.
   — Medical attention and health.
   — Studying for academic/occupational/social purposes.

At each level, and for each skill area, content is defined in terms of operations (what the learner will want to do in each area), skills (how well they will want to do these things) and text-type (what sort of texts they will need to handle). (Royal Society of Arts Examinations Board, *The Communicative Use of English as a Foreign Language*, 1983: 5-7).

The English as a Second Language Pilot Scheme 1983-84 leading to the Certificate in English as a Second Language is currently being developed for adults resident in the United Kingdom for whom English is a Second Language. In other words, in contrast with the examinations described above, it is designed for students who are second, rather than foreign language learners of English. In order to present themselves for the Certificate, candidates must complete a minimum of 100 hours tuition at an approved centre. The assessment procedure itself is in two parts. The first of these is a profile certificate, and for this students are continuously assessed throughout the duration of their course. Candidates may enter for any of the four skills assessed (Reading, Writing, Listening and Oral Interaction) and must demonstrate ability in at least three profile objectives in the target skill area. (Sample profile objectives are listed below.)

The second part of the assessment scheme is an examination, which consists of four tests in the same skills areas as listed for the profile certificate.

The following areas are suggested from which syllabuses should be developed. A minimum of five of these must be included in the syllabus of each course.

— Social interaction
— Dealing with official and semi-official bodies
— Visiting places of interest and entertainment
— Shopping and using services
— Travel
— Media
— Medical and health
— Education for self and family
— Employment
— Motoring and road safety
— Culture and religion.

There is also provision for teaching centres to suggest their own content areas.

Sample profile objectives for the certificate are as follows:

Reading:
— Understand a variety of signs and short public notices.
— Recognise where to write items of personal information on simple printed forms or questionnaires.
— Identify text and topic from such clues as layout, headings, typeface etc.
— Follow written instructions from text and diagram.

Writing:
— Fill in a form for self and family given some assistance.
— Copy short written details accurately.
— Write a simple formal letter to a known recipient.
— Demonstrate the ability to persuade, adjusting writing style to recipient.

Listening:
— Demonstrate the ability to recognise sequential, logical

and other markers.
— Identify different attitudes and emotions.
— Recognise relationship, context and topic in dialogue.
— Follow simple instructions given orally.

Oral Interaction:
— Exchange greetings and personal details with sympathetic interlocutor.
— Make appropriate apology and response.
— Open, conduct and close a brief telephone conversation.
— Explain and discuss a problem with a relevant agency.

The specifications for these two examinations have been reproduced in some detail here because they give a good idea of the way one influential examinations board is going about the task of assessing communicative performance. A number of comments can be made about the examinations themselves.

The first is that it is obvious, particularly in the case of the Certificate in ESL, that the assessment specifications and the syllabus design are intimately interrelated. In fact, the RSA has recognised that the development of examinations also entails a responsibility for syllabus specification. The link between all elements in the syllabus design process has been a constant theme throughout this paper. There is evidence that the RSA is involved in trying to come to terms with the relationship between syllabuses and examinations.

Both examinations attempt to specify communicative performance at more than one level of difficulty. The concept of difficulty, and ways of specifying difficulty have beset syllabus design, particularly since the development of communicative approaches to language teaching. In an earlier section, it was seen that, once one departs from a grammatical rationale for the selection and grading of input, the concept of difficulty becomes problematic.

In the case of the EFL examination, difficulty is specified at three different levels (Basic, Intermediate and Advanced) in terms of degrees of skill exhibited by candidates, the operations which they are required to perform and the text types they are required to produce and process. Students must nominate before the examination which level they wish to attempt.

In the examination for the Certificate in ESL, the papers themselves become progressively more difficult. Candidates need not prespecify which level they wish to attempt, and it is up to the examiner to take the candidate as far as he/she can go.

For the classroom teacher wishing to assess gains in language skills by students, the problem is to decide what sort of testing procedure to follow; whether to use standardised tests produced by someone else or whether to develop teacher-made tests. Given the increased responsibility on teachers to be more directly involved in all aspects of the syllabus design process, it would seem that teacher-made tests ought to feature more prominently in future. When the setting of objectives was discussed, it was pointed out that objectives, in specifying what the learner ought to be able to do at the end of a course of study, relate directly to testing rather than to methodology. Teachers should therefore integrate their planning of objectives and testing. The testing procedures themselves need not be all that elaborate. Informal checks on whether in fact students can do what the objectives specify may be all that is necessary. If, for example, an objective relates to the development of a core vocabulary, then some sort of vocabulary test ought to be conducted at some stage. Grids, such as those presented in Appendix B, can be readily turned into evaluation instruments. One grid is provided for each student, and cells are checked off as objectives are achieved.

While all teachers do, in fact, evaluate constantly (this evaluation may be little more than an informal monitoring of the way the class is going) there is a need for this evaluation to be more systematic. Some teachers resist more rigorous evaluation (and, for that matter, objective setting) because they are afraid that their students may be shown not to have achieved the goals that have been set. If, however, evaluation is seen as a logical and necessary part of improving teaching and learning rather than as a device for judging the teacher, then the teacher has nothing to fear. If, in fact, tests show that students have not achieved the objectives of a course, it may well be that the objectives themselves need to be modified. It is to allow this sort of modification that a process model of syllabus design has been advocated here.

As has already been mentioned, evaluation is concerned with more than testing student achievement. In order to improve teaching and learning, it is necessary, not only to gauge the success or failure to achieve objectives, but also to find out why certain results were obtained. If a given objective or set of objectives is not achieved, it is important to try and determine why. Long (1983), provides an example of how the monitoring of classroom interaction revealed a mismatch between objectives and the teaching learning process.

The need to gain more accurate insights into what goes on in the learning process, along with an awareness of the limitations of psychometric methods of measurement, has led to the development of an approach to research and evaluation which has been called 'action research'. Action research methods are particularly suitable as they are generally carried out by teachers and are specifically designed to enable the teacher/researcher to present a descriptive account of learning processes.

An early proponent of the teacher as researcher was Stenhouse (1975) who rejected the 'rational curriculum model'. For Stenhouse, the most efficacious way of improving teaching and learning was not to adopt a static model, but to get teachers to examine, reflect on and improve their current practice. He saw the central and crucial role played by the teacher, and sought ways in which this role could be enhanced. He recognised that the improvement of teaching and learning was dependent upon a closer relationship between the teacher and those aspects of curriculum development (such as evaluation) which many teachers in the past had not addressed in any systematic way. He also questioned the 'restricted professional' who is almost exclusively concerned with methodological issues maintaining that:

> I don't think this limited role and limited autonomy is a satisfactory basis for educational advance. The critical characteristics of that extended professionalism which is essential for well-founded curriculum research and development seems to me to be:
>> The commitment to systematic questioning of one's own teaching as a basis for development;
>> The commitment and the skills to study one's own teaching;
>> The concern to question and to test theory in practice by the use of those skills.
>
> To these may be added as highly desirable though perhaps not essential: a readiness to allow other teachers to observe one's work—directly through

recordings—and to discuss it with them on an open and honest basis.

In short, the outstanding characteristic of the extended professional is a capacity for autonomous professional self-development through systematic self-study, through the study of the work of other teachers and through the testing of ideas by classroom research procedures. (Stenhouse, 1975: 144).

This quote clearly reveals Stenhouse's commitment to a view of evaluation which transcends the 'rational' curriculum model, and which accords a central place to the critical self-evaluation of the classroom teacher.

Long (1983), who is also critical of a narrow approach which equates evaluation and testing, distinguishes between product evaluation (measuring what someone can do at the end of a course of training) and process evaluation. For Long, process evaluation is 'the systematic observation of classroom behaviour with reference to the theory of (second) language development which underlies the program being evaluated' (p.7). Long's position is thus very close to that of Stenhouse in identifying the classroom, and what happens there, as central to evaluation. He adds an important element, however, in making reference to the need for articulating the theory or yardstick against which one can measure what is happening in the classroom. He gives an example of a process evaluation project which revealed a mismatch between what teachers said and thought they were doing in the classroom (subscribing to a 'Natural' model of language acquisition) and what they actually did (utilised techniques more in keeping with a behaviourist model).

Kemmis and McTaggert (1982) have produced a practical guide for teachers wishing to undertake action research projects. Their *Action Research Planner* provides a set of procedures for identifying areas where improvements might be effected, and for planning, implementing and evaluating action designed to improve teaching and learning. They follow Lewin's (1946) model which sees action research as a series of spiralling steps from planning, action and observation through to reflection.

Kemmis and McTaggert maintain their focus on the practical concerns of the classroom teacher, assisting teachers in working through the four essential steps in their action research process. They also provide practical advice on how to select appropriate projects for action (for example, avoiding issues one can do nothing about) and point out that projects need not necessarily be particularly grand.

In terms of assessing current practice and striving for future improvements, it would seem that classroom based action research and evaluation is the way to go. If this is so, the major task is to sensitise teachers and provide them with the skills and tools they need to carry out research and evaluation. As indicated by Kemmis and McTaggert, it is unnecessary and inappropriate to conceive of classroom based action research in grand terms. The principle aim ought to be to make some sort of assessment of whether the objectives of the course have been achieved, and, if they have not, why this might be so. The most realistic way of improving practice is probably to select one particular area, issue or problem to work on. For instance, in a communicative classroom, one of the objectives might to be encourage more student initiated questioning of the teacher. If the evaluation of a given course reveals that the amount of student questioning is inadequate, then a possible evaluation-linked action research project would be to devise strategies for increasing this. The action research project would then move through the cycle described by Kemmis and McTaggert of planning, action, observation and reflection. This example shows how an action research orientation on the part of the teacher is an integral part of the evaluation process, and also provides a rational link with the other elements in the process model of syllabus design which forms the basis for this paper. (It may well be that as a result of the sort of action research project described above, the teacher decides that, given the resources and nature of the course it is unrealistic to expect an increase in student questioning and that the course objectives need to be modified.)

Richards (1984), takes a slightly more product orientated view of evaluation than the one presented here. He sees evaluation as being primarily concerned with estimating the degree to which the objectives of a course have been met, although he also emphasises the importance of evaluation procedures in improving rather than merely describing what goes on in the classroom. He outlines the following steps in any comprehensive evaluation procedure:

    i. set goals and objectives
    ii. decide on program-factors to be evaluated
    iii. develop criteria for deciding on success or otherwise of objectives
    iv. design instruments for assessing factors

     v. collect the necessary data
    vi. compare data with desired results
   vii. decide what was successful and what was not
  viii. prepare an evaluation report which includes recommendations for change (Richards, 1984: 22-23).

If such a model were to be adopted by an educational institution it would have to provide teachers with the necessary support for carrying out what are an exhaustive set of procedures. Such support must necessarily include skills development through in-servicing, measurement and reporting instruments and probably most important of all, the necessary time for carrying out the evaluation procedures.

14 Conclusion

This handbook contains an extended discussion of the various elements in a process model of syllabus design. I have tried to present a summary of current thinking on syllabus issues relating to each of the elements within the model. In doing so, I have emphasised those aspects which are most in keeping with a learner-centred, needs-based view of language learning and teaching.

Despite the general and rather wide ranging discussion, I hope that a number of common themes have emerged. It certainly seems to me that, despite the diversity of opinion and outlook, there is more that unites than divides those of us concerned with new directions in syllabus design. In this section, I should like to summarise what I see as the common threads.

First, and most important, there is a need for an integrated view of syllabus design and methodology. If there is a division between syllabus design and methodology, or, indeed, between the various elements in the design model itself, then problems are likely to occur. Not only should the various elements such as objectives and evaluation be planned together but there should be enough flexibility for any one element to feed back into and to influence any other.

Another important point made in the paper relates to the role of the teacher as a professional. Increasingly, teachers are being asked to take responsibility for areas of the syllabus with which, once upon a time, they were only peripherally concerned. This places greater demands on the teacher but will also bring professional rewards. An immediate problem is to convince already overworked teachers of this. If significant numbers of teachers remain unconvinced, then of course the ideas discussed in this paper will not find their way into the classroom.

Each of the syllabus design elements discussed here has one or more central concepts associated with it. In fact, these can be presented as a set of 'buzz' words. This paper is liberally sprinkled with 'objective and subjective needs', 'multidimensional input specifications', 'performance objectives', 'authentic materials and activities', 'cognitive complexity', 'staging models', 'distance learning', 'self-access', 'process evaluation', 'action research' and so on. Rather than fragmenting the field, however, they add up to a view of language learning which, though complex, does have a certain unity. For me the unifying element is the learner and his/her needs, motivations and aspirations. Our central task is to help learners master those aspects of the language they need to fulfil their own immediate and long term goals beyond language in the ways and environments that suit them best. From this perspective, we do not utilise authentic materials because they happen to be trendy at the moment or because there happen to be plenty of them lying around, but because in our professional judgment these are more likely than non-authentic materials to assist learners when they come to trying to make sense of the language they encounter in the world beyond the four walls of the classroom. In the same way, we do not develop different modes and environments because we think they might be more cost effective, but because we believe more flexible arrangements will best serve the diverse needs, learning styles and so on of the learners. For good or ill, it needs to be borne in mind that the vast majority of students do not learn English just for the fun of it, but as a tool to assist them in achieving other goals.

References

AMEP, 1984, *AMEP Handbook*. Canberra: Department of Immigration and Ethnic Affairs. Adult Migrant Education Program.

Belasco, S., 1981. Aital cal aprene las lenas estrangieras, Comprehension: The key to second language learning. In H. Winitz (ed.) *The Comprehensive Approach to Foreign Language Instruction*.

Bell, R., 1981. *An Introduction to Applied Linguistics*. London: Batsford.

Brindley, G., 1984. *Needs Analysis and Objective Setting in the Adult Migrant Education Program*. Sydney: New South Wales, Adult Migrant Education Service.

Brown, G., and **Yule, G.**, 1983. *Teaching the Spoken Language*. Cambridge: Cambridge University Press.

Candlin, C., and **Edelhoff, C.**, 1982. *Challenges: Teacher's Guide*. London: Longman.

Clark, J., and **Hamilton, J.**, 1984. *Syllabus Guidelines 1: Communication*. London: CILT.

Corbel, C., 1984. The Missing Link in Course Design. Paper presented at the Australian Federation of Modern Language Teachers Conference, September, 1984.

Diesendorf, E., Lockwood, J., and **Perkins, J.**, 1984. *The Language of Childbirth*. Sydney: New South Wales, Adult Migrant Education Service.

Gattegno, C., 1972. *Teaching Foreign Languages in Schools: The Silent Way*. New York: Educational Solutions.

Gray, M., and **Kleist, J.**, 1983. *Distance Learning Project: Course Organisation and Language Content*. Canberra: Department of Immigration and Ethnic Affairs.

Gronlund, N., 1981. *Measurement and Evaluation in Education*. New York: Macmillan.

Ingram, D., 1979. *Methodology*. Canberra: Department of Immigration and Ethnic Affairs.

Johnson, K., 1982. *Communicative Syllabus Design and Methodology*. Oxford: Pergamon.

Johnston, M., 1984. *Syntactic and Morphological Progressions in Learner English*. MS. Canberra: Department of Immigration and Ethnic Affairs.

Johnston, M., 1985. Second language acquisition research in Australia. *Prospect*, 1, 1.

Kemmis, S., and McTaggert, R., 1982. *The Action Research Planner*. Victoria: Deakin University Press.

Knowles, M., 1973. *The Adult Learner: A Neglected Species*. Houston: Gulf Publishing Company.

Krashen, S., 1981. *Second Language Acquisition and Second Language Learning*. Oxford: Pergamon.

Krashen, S., and Terrell, T., 1983. *The Natural Approach*. Oxford: Pergamon.

Lewin, K., 1946. Action research and minority problems. *Journal of Social Issues*, 2, 34-46.

Long, M., 1983. Process and product in ESL program evaluation. Paper presented at the Fifth Annual TEASOL Summer meeting, Toronto, Canada, July, 1983.

MacDonald-Ross, M., 1975. Behavioural Objectives: a critical review. In Golby et al. (eds) *Curriculum Design*.

Munby, J., 1978. *Communicative Syllabus Design*. Cambridge: Cambridge University Press.

Newmark, L. 1981. Participatory Observation: How to Succeed in Language Learning. In H. Winitz (ed.) *The Comprehension Approach to Foreign Language Instruction*.

Nunan, D., 1983. *The Developmental Language Project*. A report to the South Australian College of Advanced Education and the Adult Migrant Education Service of South Australia.

Prabhu, N., 1984. Procedural Syllabuses. In J. Read (ed.), *Trends in Language Syllabus Design*. Singapore: RELC.

Richards, J., 1984. Language Curriculum Development. *RELC Journal*, 15, 1.

Richterich, R., (ed.), 1983. *Case Studies in Identifying Language Needs*. Oxford: Pergamon.

Rivers, W., 1983. *Communicating Naturally in a Second Language*. Cambridge: Cambridge University Press.

Royal Society of Arts. 1983. *The Communicative Use of English as a Foreign Language*. London: RSA.

Royal Society of Arts. 1983-84. *English as a Second Language Pilot Scheme*. London: RSA.

Shaw, P. 1982. Ad Hoc Needs Analysis. *Modern English Teacher*, 10, 1.

Stenhouse, L., 1975. *An Introduction to Curriculum Research and Development*. London: Heinemann.

Strevens, P., 1984. What happens when someone learns a language? Paper presented at Bell Educational Trust Seminar, Bowthorpe Hall, Norwich, August, 1984.

Taba, H., 1962. *Curriculum Development: Theory and Practice*. New York: Harcourt Brace.

Terrell, T., 1982. A Natural Approach. In. R. Blair (ed) *Innovative Approaches to Language Teaching*. Rowley: Newbury House.

Trim, J., 1983. Yes, But What Do You Mean By Communication? In Brumfit, C.J. (ed.) *Learning and Teaching Languages for Communication; Applied Linguistic Perspective*. London: Centre for Information on Language Teaching and Research.

Tyler, R. 1949. *Basic Principles of Curriculum and Instruction*. Chicago: University of Chicago Press.

Valette, R., and Disick, R., 1972. *Modern Language Performance Objectives and Individualisation*. New York: Harcourt Brace.

Van Ek, J., 1975. *Threshold Level English*. Oxford: Pergamon.

Wells, G., 1981. *Learning Through Interaction: The Study of Language Development*. Cambridge: Cambridge University Press.

Widdowson, H., 1979. *Explorations in Applied Linguistics*. Oxford: Oxford University Press.

Widdowson, H., 1981. ESP In L. Selinker et al. (eds) *English for Academic and Technical Purposes*. Rowley: Newbury House.

Widdowson, H., 1983. *Language Purpose and Language Use*. Oxford: Oxford University Press.

Wilkins, D., 1976. *Notional Syllabuses*. Oxford: Oxford University Press.

Winitz, H., (ed.) 1981. *The Comprehension Approach to Foreign Language Instruction*. Rowley: Newbury House.

Yalden, J., 1983. *The Communicative Syllabus: Evolution, Design and Implementation*. Oxford: Pergamon.

Appendix A

Sample needs analysis survey form.

This form was developed for use at the Pennington Migrant Education Centre, South Australia. Students complete the form with assistance from bilingual information officers.

Date:_____ASLPR_____

                                                    L S R W

Name:_____Address:_____

Age:_____Country of Origin:_____

Family: M.S.W.D. No. of Children:_____Ages:_____

Other relatives in Australia:_____

Elsewhere:_____

Education: No. of years:_____Qualifications:_____

                Why study finished:_____

                English study:_____

Employment: Main occupation:_____

                Other jobs held:_____

                In Australia:_____

                Type of work sought:_____

Interests: e.g. hobbies, sports, leisure activities:_____

                Skills:_____

First language: _____Others spoken:_____

                                        Others studied:_____

Language learning:

A. Do you like to learn English by READING
                                    WRITING
                                    LISTENING AND SPEAK-
                                    ING
                                    OTHER

    which do you like the most?_____

B. Do you like to study grammar
                learn new words
                practise the sounds and pronunciation?

    Which do you like the most?_____

68

C. Do you like to learn English by:

_____ cassettes
_____ games
_____ talking to English speakers
_____ studying English books
_____ watching T.V.

Which is the most important (1—5) to you?_____

D. Macroskills

1. Reading:
   (a) Can you use a dictionary
   —a little _____ very well _____
   (b) What can you read in English:

                simple stories
                newspapers
                forms: bank
                       P.O.
                       C.E.S.
                advertisements: shopping
                               housing
                               employment
                bus timetables
                maps/directories
                school notes
   (c) What are the most important for you to learn now:_____

2. Writing:
   (d) Do you ever write letters
                notes to teachers
                fill in forms
   (e) Which is the most important for you to learn now:_____

3. Listening and speaking:

   _____

   (f) Who do you speak with in English?

           (g) How much do you understand?

   _____

   0 a little a lot 100%

Shop assistants
Neighbours and friends
Bus drivers
Medical people
Teachers
Employers
Others

(h) Who is it most important for you to learn to speak with now?_____

(i) Do you watch T.V.
    listen to the radio

(j) How much do you understand?

E. How do you learn best?

	No	A little	Good	Best
alone				
pairs				
small group				
class				
outside class				

F. What do you feel are the most important things for you to learn in the:
short term_____
long term_____

G. How much time is available for study now:
per day_____
per week_____

Where would you like to study:
I.L.C._____
Home_____

H. Agreement:
Length ___ / ___ / ___ to ___ / ___ / ___

How often do you want supervision:
I. Date of first supervision ___/___/___
   Comments (may include impressions of interviewer/interpreter):
J. Interviewer:_____
   Interpreter:_____
   Date:_____

Appendix B

Sample Objective/Content Grids for Three Different Teaching Contexts

Sample Objectives/Content grid for advanced reading course based on newspaper articles.

INPUT

General Objectives
1. Identifies textual relationships.
2. Identifies and demonstrates understanding of rhetorical structuring.
3. Demonstrates ability to transform textual content.

	The Razzmatazz They Call Democracy	CIA Quietly Booming	Software Sampler	Animal Liberation	Is There Life After Marriage?	Man vs Virus
Specific Outcomes						
1.1 Assigns referents to antecedents.	✓	✓	✓	✓	✓	
1.2 Identifies points of ellipsis.						
1.3 Identifies substituted information.			✓✓	✓	✓✓	
1.4 Traces identity chains.						
1.5 Identifies marked logical relationships.	✓	✓✓		✓		✓
1.6 Identifies unmarked logical relationships.	✓	✓				
1.7 Identifies text-bound synonyms.			✓		✓	✓
1.8 Identifies instances of lexical collocation.				✓		
2.1 Identifies main points in a passage.	✓	✓			✓	
2.2 Identifies type of supporting detail.	✓	✓				
2.3 Inserts additional information at an appropriate point in passage.	✓		✓			✓
2.4 Arranges list of points in order in which they appear in passage.	✓		✓			
2.5 Arranges sentences into coherent and cohesive passage.			✓	✓	✓	
2.6 Distinguishes between given and new information.			✓	✓		✓
2.7 Distinguishes between introductory, developmental and concluding paragraphs.			✓	✓		✓
3.1 Transforms content into tabular form.	✓	✓	✓	✓	✓	
3.2 Presents content in different rhetorical format.	✓		✓	✓		✓
3.3 Presents critical review of content.			✓			✓
3.4 Distinguishes between appropriate and inappropriate inferences.						

Objective/Content Grid
Adapted from RSA ESL Pilot Scheme

	Social Interaction	Dealing with official bodies	Visting places of interest and entertainment	Shopping and using services	Travel	Media	Medical and health	Education for self and family	Motoring and road safety	Culture and religion	Employment	
READING 1. Understand a variety of signs and short public notices 2. Recognise where to write items of personal information on forms 3. Extract relevant information from diagrams, maps 4. Identify text or topic from layout, headings etc. 5. Follow written instructions from text or diagram												
WRITING 1. Fill out forms for self and immediate family, given some assistance 2. Copy short written details accurately 3. Write a simple notice, note or message 4. Relay accurately an item of spoken info. in writing 5. Complete mail order payments, cheques etc.												
LISTENING 1. Demonstrate ability to recognise sequential, logical and other markers 2. Identify different emotions and attitudes 3. Recognise the essential facts of a sequence of events given orally 4. Extract factual info. from a broadcast or public service announcement 5. Convey the gist of a single message to a 3rd person												
ORAL INTERACTION 1. Exchange greetings and personal details with a sympathetic interlocutor 2. Offer and ask for help 3. Ask or respond to a number of related questions to obtain or give advice or opinion 4. Make arrangements involving time/ location 5. Give a sequence of clear oral instructions and respond to requests for clarification.												

Objective/Content Grid
Adapted from
Basic Literacy Course

	Self and Family	Shopping	Health	The home	Relationships	Getting about	Australian life	
1. UNDERSTAND CORE VOCABULARY Recognise target items in normal speech Identify pictures representing target items Name items in response to picture cues Classify objects into appropriate categories								
2. COMPREHEND BASIC FUNCTIONS Identify entities from descriptions Follow simple directions Carry out action sequence in response to instructions Respond appropriately to requests for information								
3. OBTAIN RELEVANT INFORMATION Use question forms in a way which is comprehensible Use appropriate intonation patterns Complete simple problem solving tasks								
4. DEVELOP INITIAL READING SKILLS Identify alphabet in response to aural cues Match flashcards with pictures and objects Decode words with regular CVC patterns Sight-read core vocabulary items								

D. J. WOOLMAN, GOVERNMENT PRINTER, SOUTH AUSTRALIA

F9137